10/10

Growing Up Green

Jeanne Sturm

ROURKE PUBLISHING

www.rourkepublishing.com

www.rourkepublishing.com

PHOTO CREDITS: Cover: © Katrina Brown, © Jesus Ayala, © Claudia Dewald, © Dean Turner; Title Page, 9: © ranplett; Page 5: © Galyna Andrushko; Page 6: © Bart Coenders; Page 7: © Charlybutcher; Page 8: © Lev Mel; Page 10: © vbotond; Page 11: © Jo Ann Snover; Page 12: © Lisa Fletcher; Page 13: © Alan Crawford; Page 15: © Sergiy Serdyuk; Page 16: © Duane Ellison; Page 17: © David Armentrout (top), © Cathy Yeulet (bottom); Page 18: © Nikolay Titov; Page 19: © Carmen Martínez Banús; Page 21: © Geo Martinez; Page 22: Sadeugra

Edited by Kelli L. Hicks

Cover and Interior design by Tara Raymo

Library of Congress Cataloging-in-Publication Data

Sturm, Jeanne.
 Growing up green / Jeanne Sturm.
    p. cm.
 Includes bibliographical references and index.
 ISBN 978-1-61590-301-6 (Hard Cover) (alk. paper)
 ISBN 978-1-61590-540-9 (Soft Cover)
 1. Sustainable living--Juvenile literature. 2. Green movement--Juvenile literature. I. Title.
 GE197.S78 2011
 640--dc22
                            2010009642

Rourke Publishing
Printed in the United States of America, North Mankato, Minnesota
033010
033010LP

www.rourkepublishing.com - rourke@rourkepublishing.com
Post Office Box 643328 Vero Beach, Florida 32964

Table of Contents

What Does it Mean to Grow Up Green? 4

Clean Land   6

Clean Air   14

Clean Water   20

Glossary   23

Index   24

What Does it Mean to Grow Up Green?

Growing up green means taking care of our world. It means we care for our land, our air, and our water.

Clean Land

It's important to take care of our planet by keeping it clean.

We can help by throwing away trash. But what else can we do?

We can **recycle** paper, cans, plastic, and glass.

Think Green!
Keeping old batteries out of the trash protects our water and air.

Think Green!
Others can enjoy our old toys, clothes, and books.

We can **reuse** things instead of throwing them away.

How many plastic water bottles do you use every week? Try a reusable water bottle instead.

Start a **compost pile** with grass and leaves. Add fruit and vegetable scraps. You can use it to feed your garden.

Clean Air

Burning **fossil fuels**, such as coal and oil, adds harmful **carbon dioxide** to the air. It's easy to help.

Turn off lights!

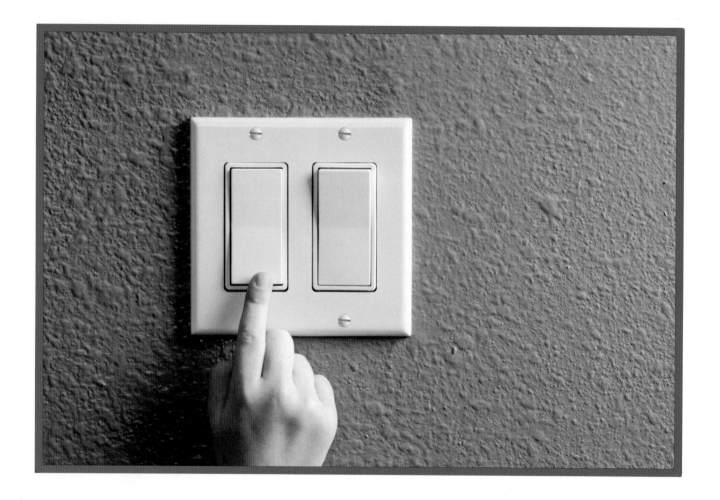

Take the bus!

Ride your bike!

Plant a tree. Trees remove carbon dioxide from the air. They also keep our homes cooler in the summer.

Reuse a Cardboard Egg Crate to Start Your Garden

- Fill the sections of an empty cardboard egg crate with soil.

- Plant seeds in the sections and water them each day.

- When the seedlings sprout, cut the sections apart and plant each one in the ground.

- The egg crate will dissolve over time as your garden grows.

Clean Water

We need clean water to drink and to grow living things. It's up to us to use water wisely.

Think Green!

Are you water wise?

- 💧 *Do you turn off the water while you are brushing your teeth?*
- 💧 *Do you take short, 5 minute showers?*

Living green means doing things that are good for the planet. What can you do to help?

RECYCLE

REDUCE

REUSE

Glossary

carbon dioxide (KAR-buhn dye-OK-side): a gas formed when fossil fuels are burned

compost pile (KOM-pohst PILE): a pile of rotting leaves, vegetable scraps, and manure that can be used to fertilize growing plants

fossil fuels (FOSS-uhl FYOO-uhlz): coal, oil, and natural gas; fuels formed from the remains of prehistoric plants and animals

recycle (ree-SYE-kuhl): use old paper, plastic, glass, and metal to make new products

reuse (ree-YOOZ): use something again

Index

carbon dioxide   14, 18

compost pile   12

fossil fuels   14

recycle   8

reusable   11

reuse   10

trash   7, 8

Websites

www.kids.nationalgeographic.com/Stories/SpaceScience/Green-tips/

www.healthy-kids-go-green.com/

www.planetpals.com

About the Author

Jeanne Sturm lives in Florida with her husband and three children. She enjoys riding her bike, reading, and quilting. She also likes to go windsurfing with her family in the Gulf of Mexico. Jeanne is planning a vegetable garden and compost pile in her back yard and looks forward to enjoying fresh vegetables and fruits.